Lessons From My Garden

By

Paula Bell

www.xulonpress.com

LESSONS FROM MY GARDEN

To everything there is a season, and a time to every purpose
under the heaven: a time to be born and a time to die;
a time to plant, and a time to pluck up
that which is planted. Ecclesiastes 3:1-2

LESSON 1

Prepare the Soil

This is the history of the heavens and the earth when they
were created, in the day the Lord God made the earth and
the heavens before any plant of the field was in the earth
and before any herb of the field had grown. For the Lord
God had not caused it to rain on the earth and there was no
man to till the ground, but a mist went up from
the earth and watered the whole face of the ground.
Gen 2:4-6

B efore God planted His garden He created the earth and provided a way for the soil to be watered. Then God planted a
garden eastward in Eden. (Gen 2:8)

Each spring we go out to assess the condition of the garden. We
begin to clear away the debris and then till the ground. As we work up
the ground we begin to plan what we will plant and where. Different
plants have different requirements for soil condition, water and sunlight. If the soil is too hard the beets will not grow underground, so
it must be soft enough to move as they expand. Kale grows up and
seems to do well in most any place.

In Matthew Jesus tells a parable about a sower and seed. Only
the seed which fell on *"good ground"* produced fruit. The seed is
the Word and we are the ground. Our hearts must be tilled; we too
must be broken so we are good ground for the seed of God's Word.
Let the Holy Spirit do the work in your life. It is only through our
brokenness that we invite God to work. When we hear the word,
if we understand it and put it to use in our lives we will bear good
fruit. *"Some a hundredfold, some sixty, and some thirty."* (Matthew
13:23) What are you waiting for? Go before the Lord and till up
the ground of your heart. Allow Him to plant the seed and expect a
wonderful harvest.

Prayer Focus:

"Create in me a clean heart, O God" Psalm 51:10a

Creator God, help me today to see the areas where I need to work. Make my heart fertile ground for the seed of your Word....

_____

_____

_____

_____

_____

_____

_____

_____

_____

_____

_____

_____

_____

_____

_____

_____

_____

_____

_____

LESSON 2

I Plant the Seeds — God Makes them Grow

*In the morning sow your seed
and in the evening do not withhold your hand:
for you do not know which will prosper, either this or that,
or whether both alike will be good. Ecclesiastes 11:6*

Once I put the seed in the ground I have no idea if it will come up or not. In fact, the seed must die in order to live. It first grows downward, forming the roots and then we begin to see the first signs of the plant above ground. I can keep it watered if it is dry but that's about it. People might say the rest depends on the weather, but who controls that? God! So you see I plant the seeds but it is God who determines if they grow.

God also has a plan and timing for your growth. You can accelerate it if you study and surrender to His leading, or you can stall it out and put it on a shelf for years by doing your own thing and ignoring those spiritual nudges.

When we first come to Christ we are hungry and God feeds us. Like the seed, we need to die to our selfish desires and be guided by the Holy Spirit. We also need roots; that happens when we study the Word on our own and let God reveal to us just what we need. When we are rooted and grounded in the Word, then the beautiful plant we are starts to emerge for others to see. Only then will we be an effective witness in the world.

Take time to plant the seed of the Word deep within your heart and continue to plant, no matter how many years you have walked with the Lord. The Word is the seed that God will use to grow a beautiful garden, that you will call a life of blessing.

Prayer Focus:

For it is God who works in you both to will and to do for His good pleasure. Phil 2:13

Father, help me to be sensitive to the seeds you have planted in my heart. As I meditate on your Word show me the things that would hinder your plans for me.....

_____

_____

_____

_____

_____

_____

_____

_____

_____

_____

_____

_____

_____

_____

_____

_____

_____

_____

LESSON 3

Tall or Large Plants have Big Roots

*But he who received the seed on stony places, this is
he who hears the word and immediately receives it with joy; yet
he has no root in himself, but endures only for a while. For when
tribulation or persecution arises because of the word, immediately
he stumbles Matthew 13:20-21*

When you plant a seed there are no roots. A seedling plant has very small roots to begin with and as the plant grows the roots develop. Plants grow down establishing their roots before they grow up. Have you ever tried to pull up a stalk of corn or maybe dug up a small tree? Have you ever thought about the roots when you pull a weed? If you think about it, the bigger the plant, the larger the root system.

Have you ever thought, I wish I had faith like Sister Ginger. Why don't I see God working in my life like that? Perhaps the people we admire in the church have developed deep roots. We must be rooted and grounded in the truth of God's Word. No matter where you are in your faith with God, getting into His Word and more importantly getting His Word into you will make your roots stronger and deeper.

We can and should study the word of God with other believers; however, it will not replace the study of the Word for ourselves. God reveals to each of us important truths for our own situation as we read and meditate on His Word. When the scripture becomes personal it is full of power to work in your life. You will know, that you know, that you know, what you believe, and you will be able to stand in the day of trial.

Grow your roots. **Our God is faithful!**

Prayer Focus:

Being confident of this very thing, that He who has begun a good work in you will complete it until the day of Jesus Christ. Philippians 1:6

Father, help me remember today that your promises are true. No matter what I am going through, I know you have a good plan for me…..

_____

_____

_____

_____

_____

_____

_____

_____

_____

_____

_____

_____

_____

_____

_____

_____

_____

LESSON 4

Tend Your Garden

Then the Lord God took the man and put him in the garden of Eden to tend and keep it. Gen 2:15

Adam and Eve were placed in a garden and told to tend it and protect it. The Word in the New King James is *'tend'*; in the King James it is *'dress'*, so I looked up *'dress'* in *Strong's Concordance* (5647). I found it means *'to work,'* which we would expect, but I also found *'worshipper.'* This is very interesting to me that as we cultivate, we render to God a service and thereby worship. When we serve God according to His purpose we perform an act of worship. We need to look at our *lives as worship,* not just the time we come together in our church for *"worship"*.

The word *'keep'* in *Strong's Concordance* (8104) means *'to put a hedge around, to guard and protect.'* Now the interesting one: it also means *'a watchman.'* We need to tend to the people and things we let in our lives and our churches. Wherever God has placed us He expects us to work and watch, to tend and keep.

You might be thinking I don't have a garden, so how does this apply to me? Tend, take care of, what God has given you. Keep your home, car, bicycle, or anything else He has placed in your care in good repair. Since our bodies are His temple we also need to keep them in good shape. Are you hoping for more money, a better job or a bigger house? Then you need to take care of the money, house or job He has already given you.

We tilled up a piece of yard for a garden many years ago and then for a time we didn't have a garden. You guessed it! In the years we did not tend the garden, the weeds and grass took over. We had to do the hard work of clearing the land all over again. It was hard, but it was worth it. It is never too late, no matter how slack you've been, to tend all that's in the garden of your life. Begin again to work and protect what God has given you!

Prayer Focus:

Work your garden you'll end up with plenty of food. Play and party and you'll end up with an empty plate. Proverbs 28:19 (The Message)

Father, show me today how my life can be truly worship to you. Reveal to me those areas that I need to watch and tend.....

_____

_____

_____

_____

_____

_____

_____

_____

_____

_____

_____

_____

_____

_____

_____

_____

_____

_____

LESSON 5

The Copy Weed

Having a form of Godliness but denying its power.
And from such people turn away.
2 Timothy 3:5

When I first planted asparagus I wasn't sure what the little tiny plants would look like. Then some plants came up green and sort of fern-like at the top, I wasn't sure if they were asparagus or not. They looked a lot like asparagus so I left them alone and in a little while the real asparagus began to grow taller and taller and I could tell the difference. My husband said they were *"copy weeds."* They looked like asparagus, but after closer observation over time, the truth was known. I also found some *"copy weeds"* in among the strawberries. They had leaves that were green and shaped very similar to the strawberry plants. How did I learn to tell them apart? By studying the actual plant!

In the church we must study the Word of God the Creator in order to determine what is real and what is a copy. Given enough time people will show themselves to be real, either true Christians or *"copies."* The scripture is clear, if they are imitations we are not to be deceived. Pull the *"copy weeds,"* separate yourself from them. This can be very difficult as our culture seems to have perfected phoniness. This is one reason we need time for careful observation. Pull too soon and you may throw away a perfectly good plant. Discernment takes time and careful attention.

Prayer Focus:

A tree is known by its fruit. Matthew 12:33

Lord Jesus, your word says we are known by our fruit, help me to look at my life through your eyes. Could I be a *"copy weed?"*

_____

_____

_____

_____

_____

_____

_____

_____

_____

_____

_____

_____

_____

_____

_____

_____

_____

_____

_____

LESSON 6

Oregano or Too Much of a Good Thing?

Everyone who competes in the games exercises
self control in all things…
1Corinthians 9:25a (New American Standard Bible)

We like oregano in our Italian dishes, so I decided to plant some in the garden. When I planted the oregano it was very small and I placed it near the strawberry plants. It grew well that first year and I cut much of it. The next spring it looked dead so I pruned it vigorously and it came out much fuller. Soon it was growing all over the place and covering part of the strawberries. We know to pull the weeds because they take nutrients from the soil and choke out the plants we want, but what about a beneficial plant?

Guess what? Too much of a good thing can be just as bad as a weed! I soon discovered that some of the strawberries were dead and others remained very small because they were all but hidden under the growing oregano.

We need balance, just like the garden. Even if something is a good thing we can't allow it to crowd out God. Service work can take over important parts of our lives and consume all our time. We must be careful that we don't become so busy doing things **for God** that we forget to spend time **with God**.

Prayer Focus:

"And you shall love the Lord your God with all your hear, with all your soul, with all your mind, and with all your strength." This is the first commandment. Mark 12:30

Lord Jesus, you gave your life for me so that I might have fellowship with you and Father God. As I reflect on this lesson help me to see where I have grown too busy and not taken time for you....

_____

_____

_____

_____

_____

_____

_____

_____

_____

_____

_____

_____

_____

_____

_____

_____

_____

LESSON 7

Plants Need Water

That He might sanctify and cleanse her
with the washing of water by the word. Ephesians 5:26

Plants need water to thrive and grow. In the book of Ephesians husbands are told to wash their wives with the *"water of the Word."* Reading the Word to your spouse is a wonderful way to feed them God's truth and help them to grow into the person God would have them be. Our spirits need the Word of God just like plants need water, for without it they become weak and die. Daily watering is recommended for a healthy spirit.

The world is a dirty place. All day long we are barraged with the world's words, images, and way of doing things. We can't keep ourselves pure, a church without *"spot or blemish,"* unless we are washed daily with God's Word.

Reading the Word daily is a discipline that may take time for you to develop; however the rewards are innumerable. God's Word truly is a life force that sustains us. As I worked in the Garden, the Holy Spirit brought to my remembrance many scriptures. He would not have been able to do this if I didn't have any Word in me. Refresh your spirit. Take a bath in the cleansing water of the Word!

Prayer Focus:

Wash me thoroughly from my iniquity, and cleanse me from my sin. Psalm 51:2

Lord of All, you are a Holy God and I must be cleansed to stand before you. As I read Your word today wash me and cleanse me from all my sins.....

_____

_____

_____

_____

_____

_____

_____

_____

_____

_____

_____

_____

_____

_____

_____

_____

_____

_____

LESSON 8

Don't Water in the Heat of the Day

*...are you unmindful or actually ignorant (of the fact) that
God's kindness in intended to lead you to repent (to change
your mind and inner man to accept God's will)*
Romans 2:4b (AMP)

The morning really had gotten away from me. I over-slept, couldn't seem to get going, had some phone calls etc. Though I usually water about nine o'clock in the morning it was noon by the time I got out to the garden. Thinking the plants would really need water on this hot day I watered them. Later in the afternoon some were yellow in spots and some seemed to be withered and brown.

Little did I realize until I saw it that if you water in the hottest part of the day, the water will literally cause the plant to burn up. You have done the opposite of what you intended.

How many of us have tried to argue someone into the kingdom? We get into the heat of the moment, the hottest part of the day, and try to put the fire out with Scripture. While the Word of God is invaluable, quoting it in an angry tone while arguing with an unbeliever will not get a good result. They will not be drawn to Christ but rather *"turned off"* by the way the message is delivered. *"Love leads to repentance."* Waiting for things to cool down will be beneficial for the plants and it will also make your witnessing more effective.

Prayer Focus:

Let all bitterness, wrath, anger, clamor, and evil speaking be put away from you, with all malice. Ephesians 4:26

Lord Jesus help me to show your love and compassion to others today. In all my encounters help me to wait on your timing....

_____

_____

_____

_____

_____

_____

_____

_____

_____

_____

_____

_____

_____

_____

_____

_____

_____

_____

_____

LESSON 9

Water Gently

To speak evil of no one, to be peaceable, gentle,
showing all humility to all men.
Titus 3:2

Too much water or too strong a stream can wash the seeds right out of the ground. Sometimes they may come up, but a little off from where they are planted. Often you never see the plant you intended to grow.

It is good to be zealous and on fire for God; however, we must use some wisdom in how we relate to others. An unbeliever will run if we try to *"hit him with everything we've got."* Too much, too fast can cause them to run from you and ultimately from God.

The Holy Spirit is a gentle teacher. He will not teach us everything at once but will show us what we need for each stage of our development. We should never try to put too much on a new believer. That's not our job! We are to show them the love of Christ, answer their questions and be there for support as the Holy Spirit leads them. They will deal with the areas of their life at a pace they can handle and in a time and manner set by God. Let them!

We couldn't handle everything God has to show us all at once, so be sensitive and allow God to work.

Prayer focus:

Good and upright is the Lord: therefore He teaches sinners in the way. Psalm 25:8

Lord, remind me today that your Holy Spirit will convict and correct others, I need only keep myself in right standing with you....

_____

_____

_____

_____

_____

_____

_____

_____

_____

_____

_____

_____

_____

_____

_____

_____

_____

_____

_____

_____

LESSON 10

Wheat and Tares

Lest in gathering the tares (weeds resembling wheat) you root up the true wheat along with it. Matthew 13:29 (AMP)

S ometimes I need to let the weeds remain until I can determine where the plant I want will come up. With asparagus, the roots are in the ground and the plant comes up year after year. Too much pulling or digging in the dirt of the asparagus bed will pull up the roots. I have to wait for the plant to break through the ground so I can see where it is okay to work and pull weeds.

In other cases the baby plants are there and I need to pull the weeds to keep them from killing the plants.

Do we recognize the weeds in our lives? Can we tell the difference between what God wants for us and what is an unbeneficial habit? Can we pull the weed or is there some reason we need to wait on God's timing? This also makes me keenly aware of what I put on the garden. Do I actually sow the weeds by putting garden dirt on the land? I bought straw from the local feed store, but I don't know where it came from or what might be in it. Maybe the weeds were in the straw.

We need to be aware of what we are allowing in our lives and the source. If we aren't careful we will have more weeds to pull than we can handle. While it is true we need to be careful what we sow into the life of others, we must also be aware of what others are sowing into our lives. If it is causing doubt, confusion or unbelief, pull the weeds and replant the Word of God.

Prayer Focus

For God has not given us a spirit of fear, but of power and of love and of a sound mind. 2 Timothy 1:7

Lord as I walk through today help me to remember confusion is not of you. Show me what thoughts are beneficial and help me to cast down all those that are not of you…..

_____

_____

_____

_____

_____

_____

_____

_____

_____

_____

_____

_____

_____

_____

_____

_____

_____

_____

_____

LESSON 11

I Get What I Plant

"For whatever a man sows,
that and that only is what he will reap."
Galatians 6:7 (AMP)

This may sound a little silly but if I want tomatoes I need to plant tomatoes. Putting corn seed in the ground won't produce tomatoes. We know this when we talk about plants so why is it so hard to understand that if we are negative and angry all the time, that's what we get back? If you constantly mistreat people then why are you outraged when someone is less than kind to you?

God's principles for our lives reach far beyond the obvious. When I changed how I treated others I began to notice a difference in how they treated me. If you sow kindness you will reap kindness. When I stopped to realize this person I didn't particularly like is also a child of God, forgiven and loved just like me, it changed the way I saw them and the way I treated them.

If you need a financial blessing, give. Maybe you have a loved one who is struggling and you have prayed and you just can't help and you don't know what to do. Help someone! Be the person who helps the loved ones of others. Guide *them* towards Christ. Sow what you what to receive in your life and watch God work!

Prayer Focus:

...Those who plow iniquity and sow trouble reap the same. Job 4:8b

Lord, when I get upset am I sowing or reaping? Help me to see what I am responsible for in my life, did I say....

_____

_____

_____

_____

_____

_____

_____

_____

_____

_____

_____

_____

_____

_____

_____

_____

_____

_____

Lesson 12

Never Plant More Garden Than Your Wife Can Hoe!

Now he who received seed among the thorns is he who hears the word; and the cares of this world, and the deceitfulness of riches, choke the word, and he becomes unfruitful. Matthew 13:22

When I first started my garden, my husband would use our rotor tiller to break up the ground and then he'd help me with the planting. As he was still working a full time job, I did most of the weeding. When his friends would ask how he kept the garden so nice he would say; *"Don't plant more garden than your wife can hoe!"*

How is your schedule? Are you over-loaded and overwhelmed? Maybe you have too big a garden. If that's the case, don't take on more! Sometimes we take on things because we know we can do the task, or we want to do the task for personal reasons. Maybe we never learned to say 'no.' After all, *no isn't a four letter word!*

The question is, did God ask us to do it? What is it that God wants from us at this time? When we are working on things God has purposed for us to do, there is an ease and a peace. God always equips us for a task He assigns. It is not always easy, but there is peace and joy in our spirit. We know we are moving in what God has called us to do.

When we get overloaded there is no peace. We're stressed and irritated by the littlest inconvenience. In this state how could we possibly give our best to God or be an effective witness to the world? The world is already stressed out; they don't want more. So we must learn to balance life and move in what God has for us.

Prayer Focus:

He has shown you, O man, what is good; and what does the Lord require of you but to do justly, to love mercy, and to walk humbly with your God? Micah 6:8

Lord Jesus, show me what is in Your plan for today and help me to let everything else go…

LESSON 13

Declare — Confess the Word

*If you have faith as a mustard seed, you will **say** to this mountain, move from here to there and it will move; and nothing will be impossible for you Matthew 17: 20*

Death and life are in the power of the tongue, and those who love it will eat its fruit. Proverbs 18:21

O ver and over again as I worked in the garden I said *"Lord your Word says, he who tills the ground shall not go hungry, so I'm believing that you will bless this garden with abundance so that I can feed my family and have plenty to share with others."* This was my paraphrase of *Proverbs 28:19* and as I worked I declared it over and over. I declared the Word when the garden looked good. I declared the Word when I wasn't sure anything would grow. I believed that if I worked, God would bless, even though I didn't know what I was doing. As I worked I kept on believing that God would make things grow in spite of me and He did! The garden grew and produced a crop even in the drought year when the wells all over the Eastern Shore were going dry and I didn't water much. **God is faithful to His Word!**

God's words are containers of power. He spoke our world into existence. When we find a scripture that shows us God's will for our situation and declare it great things happen. We are in agreement with God and when we declare His Word over our lives He brings it to pass.

To paraphrase; **you *will* have what you say!** The words coming out of your mouth will influence your life for good or evil so why not declare God's Word and receive His blessings in your life? **God's word does not return void, begin declaring it today!**

Prayer Focus:

So shall My word be that goes forth from my mouth; it shall not return to me void, but it shall accomplish what I please, and it shall prosper in the thing for which I sent it. Isaiah 55:11

Creator God, let all the words of my mouth be your words....

_____

_____

_____

_____

_____

_____

_____

_____

_____

_____

_____

_____

_____

_____

_____

_____

_____

_____

LESSON 14

Pray

Pray without ceasing. 1 Thessalonians 5:17

A few years ago we were experiencing a drought. Many people in the area had their wells go dry including a couple on our street. Because of this I was afraid to put much water on the garden, fearful our well would go dry also. However, in spite of this my garden was mostly green and yielded good crops.

People would look at it and ask why my garden was green, saying *"mine doesn't look like this."* My answer was always the same *"Do you pray when you pull weeds?"* They would give me that look that said *"are you kidding?"* I explained that as I worked in the garden I prayed and talked with God. I gave Him thanks and asked him to bless the land and the plants, that I might have enough to eat and some to share. I did this day after day and God was faithful. The garden produced enough that we ate, I gave some away to friends and neighbors and some went in the freezer. My garden gave me a way to give God glory and open up conversations with others about the power of prayer.

Prayer is a conversation with God. He cares about every aspect of our lives. Have you talked with Him today? Take some time now to say a prayer and listen for His voice.

Prayer Focus:

And when He had sent the multitudes away, He went up on the mountain by Himself to pray. Now when evening came, He was alone there. Matthew 14:23

Here I am Lord I want to spend some time with you. As I wait please speak to me about….

_____

_____

_____

_____

_____

_____

_____

_____

_____

_____

_____

_____

_____

_____

_____

_____

_____

_____

LESSON 15

Give God the Glory

Render therefore to Caesar the things that are Caesar's and to God the things that are God's Matthew 22:21

I truly can't say I made the garden grow. I know I really didn't make the beauty I see when I look at it. The praise belongs to God. He created the earth, the plants, the seeds, the rain, and the sunlight. In obedience I worked the land, planted the seeds, watered when needed and the plants grew.

I did not look at the land and say, "*I wish God would put a garden here.*" That is true, but I only did a part. When we realize we can do nothing in ourselves and all that we have comes from God, it changes our perspective.

Giving God the glory and praise for what He has done in our lives is a sweet- smelling sacrifice to Him. He loves us, and when we acknowledge Him it opens the door for blessings to flow in our life. Our walk with the Lord is all about relationship.

When we give Him the glory for all He has done it allows others to get to know Him and they begin to hope He will work in their lives, too. Share your faith with others. Let the glory plant new seeds in the lives of all those around you.

Prayer Focus:

Give unto the Lord the glory due to His name... Psalm 29:2a

Lord, give me a new boldness as I tell others about all you have done for me. (Begin with a list of those things now)

_____

_____

_____

_____

_____

_____

_____

_____

_____

_____

_____

_____

_____

_____

_____

_____

_____

_____

_____

LESSON 16

Give Thanks

Giving thanks always for all things to God the Father in the name of our Lord Jesus Christ. Ephesians 5:20

I must be honest, I can't bring myself to thank God for the weeds in my garden; however, I am very thankful for the strength to pull them. I have been diagnosed with Fibromyalgia and Arthritis, but God has been working mightily in my life and I believe He will heal me completely. As time passes I see myself getting better and better. Tasks that once caused great pain for days are now easier to do with no lasting effects. So, I am truly thankful that I can now pull the weeds and not be in pain afterwards. This is only possible by the grace of God!

I also thank Him for the sunshine that lifts my spirit. I thank Him for the gentle breeze that cools me as I work. I thank Him for how beautiful the garden looks. I thank Him for the song of the birds to keep me company. To me God is very present in the garden as I am surrounded by His handiwork and the beauty of His creation. Thank you Lord for eyes to see, ears to hear and strength to do the work.

What do you have to be thankful for? If it's a bad day you may have to think hard but you *can* find something. Begin thanking Him for the smallest of things and grow your list to the point that you are truly thankful for everything.

Prayer Focus:

Oh give thanks to the Lord, for He is good! For His mercy endures forever. 1 Chronicles 16:34

Lord I want to thank you for...

_____

_____

_____

_____

_____

_____

_____

_____

_____

_____

_____

_____

_____

_____

_____

_____

_____

_____

LESSON 17

Practice First Fruits

*The first of the first fruits of your land you shall bring into
the house of the Lord your God… Exodus 23:19a*

In the Old Testament the Israelites were instructed to bring the first of the harvest to the temple to offer to God. Do we give God the first of what we receive? How often do we bring what is left after we have done all the things we wanted? I decided that I could honor God with the first of the fruits from the garden by giving them away to others. Each year I give of the first of the strawberries; as they are the first thing to come on and I have never been disappointed with what I got to enjoy later. As other crops are ready I give some of them away, also.

After giving away some, I harvest, enjoy, and store for winter. Even then sometimes there is still some to share. When we follow God's way of doing things we are never disappointed!!!

Many people don't want to hear about tithing, but it is a today way of *'first fruits'*. Before I pay bills or shop, I write a check for ten percent of that week's income. Take God's portion out first. This is the principle of *'first fruits'* and God blesses it and multiplies it. When we honor God first, there is always enough to meet our needs. Try it for yourself and see if God doesn't pour out a blessing on you.

Prayer Focus:

Honor the Lord with your possessions, and with the first fruits of all your increase: so your barns will be filled with plenty and your vats will overflow with new wine. Proverbs 3:9-10

Lord today I want to make a commitment to you, to give you the first of my income, my time....

_____

_____

_____

_____

_____

_____

_____

_____

_____

_____

_____

_____

_____

_____

_____

_____

_____

_____

LESSON 18

Rest

And on the seventh day God ended His work which He had done; and He rested on the seventh day from all His work which He had done. Genesis 2:2

There is a rhythm and a balance in nature. We need to work and we need to rest. The ground needs to rest also, in order to keep producing. The nutrients in the soil need time to replenish. I have a small garden but I still practice crop rotation. Each year I move things around so I'm not growing the same thing in the same place all the time.

I work six days and for the most part I rest on Sunday. I'm not so sure we need to argue over what day the Sabbath is, so much as we need to observe the principle of rest. We need a day to rest our physical bodies and renew our minds and spirits. Take time for God, family and activities you enjoy, break the routine. Give your work life a day off.

Life needs balance. If you have no time for friends and family you are out of balance. If all your time is consumed by others and there is no time for you, YOU need a break. Jesus left the crowds and went to the mountains to be alone with God. If Jesus needed some down time to be refreshed, what makes us think we don't? Sometimes we feel we can't slow down because there is so much to do, but God invented time and He will help you complete the things that need to be done. **Let it go**. You were never in charge, anyway. His presence soothes, comforts, settles, consoles, and quiets us. **Rest in the Lord!**

Prayer Focus:

*And He said; "My presence will go with you and I will **give** you rest." Exodus 33:14*

Father, let me remember that you are with me today. No matter what is going on I can trust you and be at rest...

_____

_____

_____

_____

_____

_____

_____

_____

_____

_____

_____

_____

_____

_____

_____

_____

_____

LESSON 19

Little by Little

And the Lord your God will drive out those nations before you little by little; you will be unable to destroy them at once, lest the beast of the field become too numerous for you. Deut 7:22

Each year the garden gets better. The soil has improved as we have worked it with the tiller and added compost. The weeds and grass are finally slowing down; we have pulled and pulled. We even tilled up more to expand the space after we got the first section under control. We have worked with what we could manage and then added a little more as we went along. Today it is a beautiful space and big enough to meet our needs without totally overwhelming us. If we had started with this size I would never have been able to keep up and the weeds would have been too numerous for me.

We grow as Christians the same way. We come to accept our Lord and Savior Jesus Christ and there is a change. Then as He works in our lives more change happens. The indwelling of the Holy Spirit brings understanding as we study and conviction comes on us when we start to stray from the path God has in His purpose. The transformation is slow; we can't deal with everything all at once. God in His wisdom transforms us little by little until the process is complete.

I will probably never be "weed-free," but I believe I am being transformed into the image of Christ. For every believer, this process will continue until the day He returns. What we need most is to be in the process, ever moving forward, on this wonderful journey.

Prayer Focus:

But we all, with unveiled face, beholding as in a mirror the glory of the Lord, are being transformed into the same image from glory to glory, just as by the Spirit of the Lord. 2 Corinthians 3:18

Thank you Lord, that you are still working on me! May I be transformed little by little each day...

_____
_____
_____
_____
_____
_____
_____
_____
_____
_____
_____
_____
_____
_____
_____
_____

LESSON 20

Peas Need Support

*Rejoice with those who rejoice,
and weep with those who weep. Romans 12:15*

W e planted peas in the garden and although they were supposed to be a bush type and not get very tall, they got tall enough to fall over. Peas have these tiny tendrils that need to hold on to something to keep the plant upright. In the absence of a string or something to climb on they grab on to each other and pull each other down.

How many new Christians have you known (or maybe it's you) who have tried holding on to the world while starting a new life in Christ? If the Body of Christ doesn't come alongside and give support, then the world will pull them down. We are called to be there supporting one another in good and bad, staying connected and upholding one another. Without the love and support of other Christians; we grab onto those around us who pull us down.

Are you struggling in your walk? Who do you have surrounding you that you can grab onto? We need the Body of Christ! God established a support system for us when He instructed the older (those with more time in the things of God) to teach the younger (new to the Christian life, not a matter of age.) We need support, and we will seek comfort from those around us. Be careful who you're hanging out with. Are they supporting you as you grow in Christ helping you to grow green and tall, or are they pulling you down toward the earth and causing your leaves to yellow and your body to bend and twist?

Perhaps you think, " *I don't need church; I can worship God anywhere. I love nature I'll worship in the park or on the lake.*" We can worship God anywhere, but we must be careful not to isolate ourselves from other believers because when the storms of life come, and they will, we, like the peas, will be looking for something to hold onto.

Prayer Focus:

Not forsaking the assembling of ourselves together, As is the manner of some; but exhorting one another and so much the more as you see the Day approaching. Hebrews 10:25

Lord, show me someone to encourage today...

_____

_____

_____

_____

_____

_____

_____

_____

_____

_____

_____

_____

_____

_____

_____

_____

_____

_____

Little Foxes and Big Ground Hogs Spoil the Garden

Catch us the foxes, the little foxes, that spoil the vines:
for our vines have tender grapes. Song of Solomon 2:15

Although I live in more of a town setting than a country one, the back property line had become overgrown with some brush. Across from the neighbor's vacant lot was a little stretch of woods. When the kale began to produce nice tender leaves I noticed them disappearing. Then I began to see tomatoes on the ground with a bite taken out of them.

One day I surprised the culprit! It was a ground hog and a big one, about 30 lbs. He was as big as my dog. As I approached he ran and hid under a small shed near the garden. I could see him peeking out watching me as if to say, *"Go back in the house, I wasn't finished with my breakfast."* Now I don't mind sharing but he was eating ALL the kale! The whole row would be mowed down at one time. He was also ruining the tomatoes before they could ripen.

Left unchecked, all the work in the garden would only profit the ground hog. We had to protect our garden from the harm he was doing, but I really didn't want to destroy him. The solution — Put up a fence!

Sometimes we have people or influences that spoil our lives. They seem to pull the rug out from under us just as things start going well. Perhaps we need a fence, or at least a good boundary. We don't want to harm others but at the same time we **cannot** allow them to destroy us or our walk with the Lord. Set appropriate boundaries for your life.

Prayer Focus:

When the Most High divided their inheritance to the nations. When He separated the sons of Adam, He set the boundaries of the peoples according to the number of the children of Israel. Deuteronomy 32:8

Most High God, you are a God of order and peace. Show me those areas where I need stronger boundaries, and give me the courage to set them...

_____

_____

_____

_____

_____

_____

_____

_____

_____

_____

_____

_____

_____

_____

_____

_____

_____

LESSON 22

Check Your Borders

Prepare yourself and be ready, you and all your companies
that are gathered about you; and be a guard for them.
Ezekiel 38:7

Anything just outside the fence has a way of creeping in. We cleared a space for my garden and worked the land. The planting began and the garden seemed to take shape. To mark it off from the yard we put some landscape timbers around it. Next, we needed a fence and so we bought some chicken wire and put it around the landscape timbers. This didn't seem right so we moved the timbers to the outside. This was yard and we didn't work it up or pull weeds or grass. Then the grass and weeds began to grow through the spaces in the chicken wire and come up under it. Now I had a very difficult time trying to get the weeds out of the wire and the garden.

If my life is like my garden then I must ask, what is just outside the fence? What things am I sort of dabbling in that maybe aren't good for me? Do I go places with others that I'm not really comfortable with because my friends are there? How many times do we say, *"Just this one time won't hurt anything."* Excuses like that can be a sign that we need to check our motives, and our heart. What is just outside the fence that we don't want to take the time or the hard work to get rid of?

Life is not easy, but we must be diligent to guard our hearts. We are responsible for what we let into our lives. Be careful you don't have things that will harm you, creeping in through the holes in your fence.

Prayer Focus:

Keep your heart with all diligence, for out of it spring the issues of life Proverbs 4:23

Today Lord, show me where I have holes in my fence...

_____

_____

_____

_____

_____

_____

_____

_____

_____

_____

_____

_____

_____

_____

_____

_____

Pick the Blossoms — Grow the Plant

*Not a novice lest being puffed up with pride he fall into the
same condemnation as the devil. I Timothy 3:6*

The first year you put strawberry plants in the ground they are mostly a root with a little green. As the leaves come out, you may get blossoms and berries on that little plant. It is better to pull the blossom off so the resources aren't spent in making fruit that first year but in growing and establishing the plant. The next year a larger, stronger, plant produces many more, as well as much nicer berries.

"Lay hands suddenly on no man. " (KJV) Grow the plant. Many times we try to place new believers in places of responsibility to keep them coming to church and often there is a negative consequence. We need to grow the disciple before placing them in a place of responsibility and expecting them to produce good fruit.

Without good roots plants can't grow strong and they either don't produce or the fruit is small. If you are a new believer, may I caution you to study, observe and learn before you go off trying to minister. You need the root of God's Word and prayer. You also need a support system. Share your faith when you can, but go slowly into offices or ministries of the church. God's timing is perfect and you'll know when you are ready.

Prayer Focus:

Do not lay hands on anyone hastily, nor share in other people's sins; keep yourself pure. I Timothy 5:22

Creator God you know just when each plant is ready for harvest and you know when I am ready to do all the things you have planned for me....

_____

_____

_____

_____

_____

_____

_____

_____

_____

_____

_____

_____

_____

_____

_____

_____

_____

_____

LESSON 24

Follow the Shade

For My yoke is easy and My burden is light. Matthew 11:30

I have fair skin and burn easily, so working very long in the hot sun is not good for me. At my stage of life I also overheat quickly and want to quit. The placement of my garden allows the sun to move over it in varying degrees as the day progresses. There is total sun in the middle of the day, but if I work in the morning or the late afternoon I can find a shady spot to work, and move with the shade as the sun moves. This makes the area less hot and if God provides a breeze I'm in really great shape.

The Holy Spirit will make our life and work for God much easier if we learn to follow His leading. We don't have to struggle so hard if we listen for the gentle leading of the Holy Spirit and follow Him. The Holy Spirit will show us when, where, and how. We don't have to do everything the hard way.

Prayer Focus:

But the Helper, the Holy Spirit, whom the Father will send in My name, He will teach you all things and bring to your remembrance all things that I said to you. John 14:26

Holy Spirit I yield to you today, teach me....

_____

_____

_____

_____

_____

_____

_____

_____

_____

_____

_____

_____

_____

_____

_____

_____

_____

_____

_____

_____

LESSON 25

Being Connected to My Creator Brings Peace

*And the Lord God formed man of the dust of the ground,
and breathed into his nostrils the breath of life;
and man became a living being. Genesis 2:7*

One of my friends says there is something spiritual about being in the garden. I must agree with her. There in my garden with my hands in the warm soil I feel a special closeness to God. Mankind was made from the dust of the earth and then placed in a garden. In the evening, God came to walk and talk with him.

In the early morning, when it's cool and before the cares of the day weigh heavily on my mind, I like to go to the garden and talk with God. It was during these special times with the Lord that He gave me the idea for this book. I began to take a little note pad to the garden to write down all the things He was showing me. The ideas just began to flow, faster than I could write them down. There was no guessing, no doubt, no struggle. God was giving me this book and I had peace about it.

God wants to talk to all of us and if we will get quiet we can hear Him. There is a peace that I cannot explain when I'm in God's presence. Jesus said *"My peace I leave with you."* Find your quiet place today. Just sit and be connected to your creator. If you will make yourself available to Him, Jesus will come and give you His peace. Shalom.

Prayer Focus:

Peace I leave with you, My peace I give to you; not as the world gives do I give to you. Let not your heart be troubled, neither let it be afraid. John 14:27

Creator God may I begin each day in your presence, creating a strong bond that will stay with me always. As I go through my work today help me to feel your peace...

_____

_____

_____

_____

_____

_____

_____

_____

_____

_____

_____

_____

_____

_____

_____

_____

_____

_____

LESSON 26

Praise Makes Work More Enjoyable.

*I will bless the Lord at all times: his praise shall
continually be in my mouth. Psalm 34:1*

There are only two times to praise the Lord, when you feel like it and when you don't! Praising when you feel down or discouraged, is an act of the will. When I have weeds to pull, I praise; when I put the seeds in the ground, I praise; when there is no rain, I praise; when God waters the garden for me, I praise. When the birds eat the strawberries, I praise. When I'm tired of working, I praise. When I look out in the morning or evening and see the beauty of the garden, I praise.

God is the Creator and He is worthy of our praise. I have discovered that it is impossible to praise and stay angry or disappointed! Praise will lift you out of any bad mood. It doesn't make your problems go away but it does refresh your spirit so you can cope. Often the solution to the problem comes during times of praise and worship.

As I work I like to sing praise songs. The songs make my spirit soar, the work seems easier and the next thing I know it is done and I have had a good time doing it. What are you facing today? Put on some praise music or sing it for yourself and get to work. Praise your way through your day and feel the presence of the Lord. Your spirit, body, and soul will thank you!

Prayer Focus:

Praise the Lord for the Lord is good; sing praises to His name, for it is pleasant. Psalm 135:3

How Great is our God! Today I will tell of the awesome greatness of my lord...

LESSON 27

Don't Go it Alone Get Help

Where there is no counsel, the people fall; but in the multitude of counselors there is safety. Proverbs 11:14

New portions of the garden were very difficult to work on, so I had to ask my husband to till them for me. We soon discovered it was more productive and a lot more fun if we worked on it together. I needed his strength and he needed my determination to have a beautiful garden.

I really didn't know what I was doing so I began to get information on organic gardening from books, magazine, websites and fellow gardeners. Some of the farmers I talked to didn't use organic methods but they still told me things about plants, things that were helpful. When we listen to others we can decide what is wisdom for us and what isn't but don't discount anyone because we can learn from everyone.

One *"old timer,"* said that plants need to struggle a little. "Why," I asked? "Because it is in the struggle that they develop deep roots," he said. "If you water the corn too much it doesn't develop deep enough roots to support the plant and the stalks fall over when the ears of corn begin to appear."

Our trials and temptations give our faith its roots. When we struggle, not being able to easily solve our problems, we learn to trust God. We learn to seek the wisdom of those who have a deeper faith and as God works out His will in our lives we learn to trust Him more. For us to get our roots down deep enough to stand we have to learn to trust that God is faithful, so we struggle. God does not let us go it alone; we have others of the faith and the assurance that God is right here with us.

Prayer Focus:

When you pass through the waters, I will be with you; and through the rivers, they shall not overflow you: when you walk through the fire, you shall not be burned;
nor shall the flame scorch you. Isaiah 43:2

I am thankful Lord Jesus that you never leave us or forsake us. Please be with me and help me today as I ....

_____

_____

_____

_____

_____

_____

_____

_____

_____

_____

_____

_____

_____

_____

_____

_____

_____

LESSON 28

Look to the Ant

Go to the ant, you sluggard! Consider her ways, and be wise, which having no captain, overseer, or ruler, provides her supplies in the summer and gathers her food in the harvest. Proverbs 6:6-8

Take the bounty God blesses you with and store some up for later. Yes, believe God will supply, but don't be wasteful. Share, give to others and then set some aside for the winter. How good strawberry jam tastes on a hot biscuit in the cold of winter! Pickles, relish, green beans, squash, beets, and tomatoes for sauce and soup, are wonderful to have in the freezer or pantry. When I store the bounty of summer, in the winter when the cost of heat is high, I can eat out of the pantry and spend less at the grocery store. God provides, we do our part, and all year long we have good things to eat!

What are you doing with the provisions God has given you? Do you spend your paycheck before you get it? Look to the Ant and set some aside each week for those little emergencies that pop up at the most inopportune times.

Work with whatever talent the Lord has given you. Is there a particular job you want but haven't been able to find? Work at something, get busy. Often people who have jobs are the ones to whom companies offer new opportunities.

God asks us to be good stewards of what He has given us, and if we haven't taken care of or been thankful for what we have, He doesn't give us more. Get busy making the most of what God has blessed you with!

Prayer Focus:

The earth is the Lord's, and all its fullness, the world and all those who dwell there in. Psalm 24:1

Lord, help me to see that all I have is Yours, and to be a better steward of all that you have given me...

_____

_____

_____

_____

_____

_____

_____

_____

_____

_____

_____

_____

_____

_____

_____

_____

_____

_____

LESSON 29

God Feeds the Birds

Delight yourself in the Lord and
He will give you the desires of your heart.
Psalm 37:4 (NIV)

God knows that the birds like strawberries and the rabbits like lettuce. He also knows that I like blackberries a lot and they are expensive at the grocery store so I buy maybe one or two little packs at the store in a year.

Some people put a net over their strawberries so the birds can't get to them, but for some reason I didn't. After all, they didn't eat much, just a few here and there, so no real harm. There were enough for the birds and me.

After a couple of years I noticed a blackberry vine growing by the pine tree in the front yard. It was small but the berries were tasty! I asked my neighbor if she had seen them just come up like that before and if she thought wild berries were safe to eat. Her reply really surprised me, "*Mr. Welch down the street had black-berry vines for a number of years. The birds must have eaten some and dropped the seeds in your yard.*" You see they weren't really "*wild.*" God had the birds plant them for me and then He took care of them so they would come up!

If you think about it, I bet you could find something that you wanted that sort of just showed up or happened unexpectedly. God knows what we need and He also knows what we want. When we honor Him in our lives He delights in blessing us with both!

Prayer Focus:

And my God shall supply all your need according to His riches in glory by Christ Jesus. Philippians 4:19

Today Lord may I open my eyes to see all the wonderful things you have provided for me...

_____

_____

_____

_____

_____

_____

_____

_____

_____

_____

_____

_____

_____

_____

_____

_____

_____

_____

_____

LESSON 30

Not All Cucumbers Make
Good Pickles

*And He Himself gave some to be apostles, some prophets,
some evangelists, and some pastors and teachers.*
Ephesians 4:11

As I worked in the garden this year I was reminded of a time when I was a young wife and mother. I was trying my hand at canning and preserving because I was at home and my husband worked on commission selling building material, so in the spring and summer we had money and in the winter we didn't.

I made jam with berries I picked and canned tomatoes I bought cheap at the packing house. These projects went well and I thought pickles would be good in the winter, too. I purchased cucumbers from a local farmer and sliced and brined for weeks, just as the recipe said, then canned them. Upon opening them the taste wasn't awful but the pickles were like cooked veggies. No snap, no crunch! I thought maybe putting them in the refrigerator would help, but you guessed it, now I just had cold over-cooked veggies. Little did I know there are cucumbers called pickling cukes. I thought all cucumbers were like the ones I had seen in salad or at the grocery store.

Now I plant pickling cukes and I'm happy to say my bread and butter pickles are pretty good. The cukes aren't bad in a salad, either. In the Body of Christ we are not all intended to be pastors, evangelists, or missionaries. God has given each of us special talents and a place in the body. Who would want to be a pickle if you weren't meant to be one? Don't try to have a ministry like anyone else, just find out what kind of cucumber you are and be happy doing just what you were meant to do. The Body of Christ needs all of us to fulfill the plan of God here on the earth.

Prayer Focus:

For as we have many members in one body, but all the members do not have the same function, so we being many, are one body in Christ, and individually members of one another. Romans 12:4-5

Today Father I want to *"Bloom where I'm planted."*

_____

_____

_____

_____

_____

_____

_____

_____

_____

_____

_____

_____

_____

_____

_____

_____

_____

_____

_____

LESSON 31

God Recycles! The Lesson of Compost

But as for you,
you meant evil against me;
but God meant it for good, Genesis 50:20a

Sometimes the plants die without producing any crop and sometimes they die when the harvest is done. Either way, they appear to be beyond any further use.

We, too, at times seem to be of no use to anyone. We're too young or we're too old. We have too much experience or not enough experience. Sometimes we just make bad choices and have a mess to clean up.

As I was pulling up some of the plants, and pruning leaves off of others to put in the compost pile it struck me, just like the dead garden waste can be turned into something useful that will improve the soil of the garden, my mistakes are taken by God and made useful again. The way He has worked and brought me through my bad choices is a powerful testimony to others so they too can begin again and have a good life.

God doesn't waste anything! Whatever you're going through He will recycle it into something good. *Welcome to the compost pile!* Thank God He isn't finished with us yet.

Prayer Focus:

For I know the thoughts that I think toward you, says the Lord, thoughts of peace and not of evil, to give you a future and a hope. Jeremiah 29:11

Father help me to remember that You have a plan for me, as I sit in Your presence guide and direct me back to the path You have chosen for me....

_____

_____

_____

_____

_____

_____

_____

_____

_____

_____

_____

_____

_____

_____

_____

LESSON 32

Sometimes Things Look Dead

O death where is thy sting,
o grave where is thy victory? 1 Corinthians 15:55 (KJV)

It was a rough winter this year. The snow came in feet instead of inches; the little pecan trees and the blueberry bushes we set out last summer seemed to get lost. Then the thaw came and they were in a lake of water. When spring finally broke everything was brown and lifeless. I wondered if they had survived. Then just as the days began to grow warm I could see the first hint of green. The trees were making leaves and little buds were forming. Wow! They were alive after all!

"O death where is thy sting, swallowed up in victory" Praise God that we come out of the death of our personal winters into new victories and new springs in our life. If you seem to be in a hard spot, if your winter is cold, dreary and long, hold on to the Word. Keep your faith strong! Spring is just around the corner.

As the last trumpet sounds, all our winters will end and ultimately our new life will be in a new and resurrected body! Thanks be to God!

Prayer Focus:

"While the earth remains, seedtime and harvest, cold and heat, winter and summer, and day and night shall not cease." Genesis 8:22

Thank you Lord that for every winter in my life there is a spring...

_____

_____

_____

_____

_____

_____

_____

_____

_____

_____

_____

_____

_____

_____

_____

_____

_____

_____

_____